In this book you can find 20 different illustrations to color and some calm words.

Each illustration was designed by hand. Their structure mirrors that of life, universe and space. The illustrations are fantastic from another world. Coloring them will take you to another universe.

So take a break from the fast-paced stresses of your own life, take a deep breath, turn on your favorite music, grab colored pencils, gel pens or markers and dive into a relaxing coloring journey. Coloring has been shown to aid in relaxation. It can help to remove from your mind all problems and even help to solve them.

Copyright © Yana Krukovets

… You are in a big noisy city. Everyone is running somewhere, everyone is thinking about something, talking about something…

But stop! Look at the flower bed near the store. Smell the flowers, look at their beauty. And then the world stopped for a second or even for the three …

Happiness is near, beauty is near, relax is here …

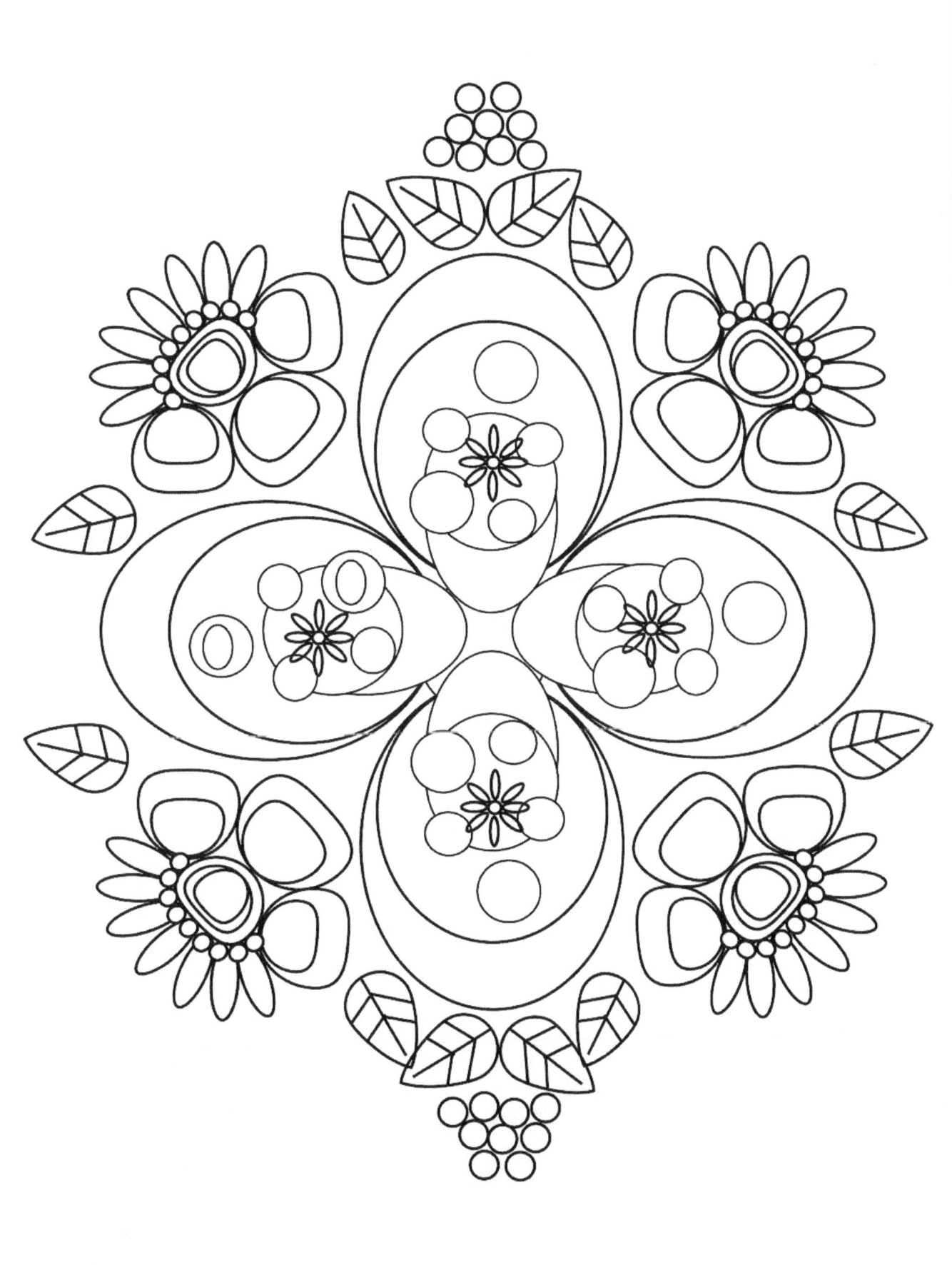

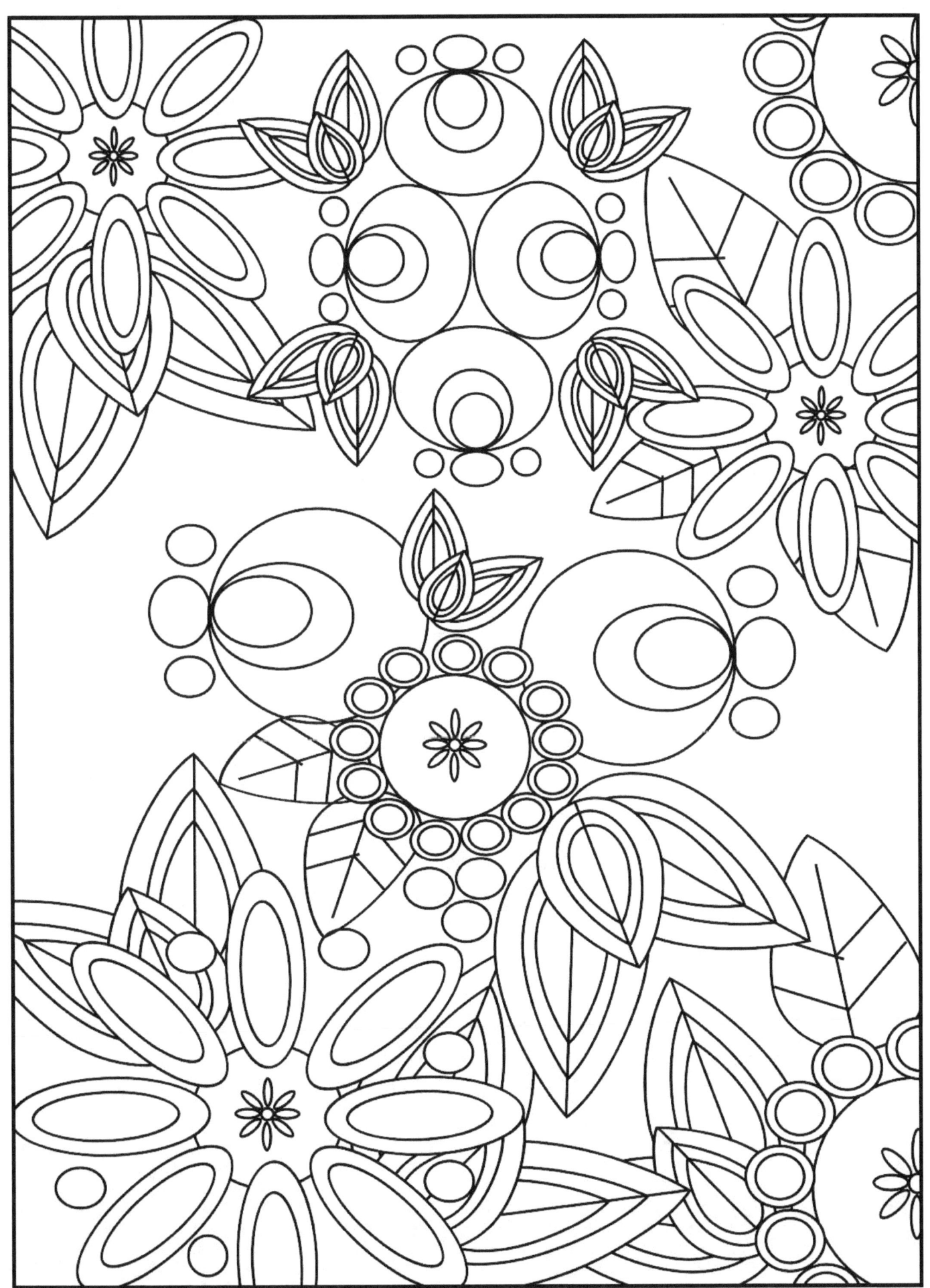

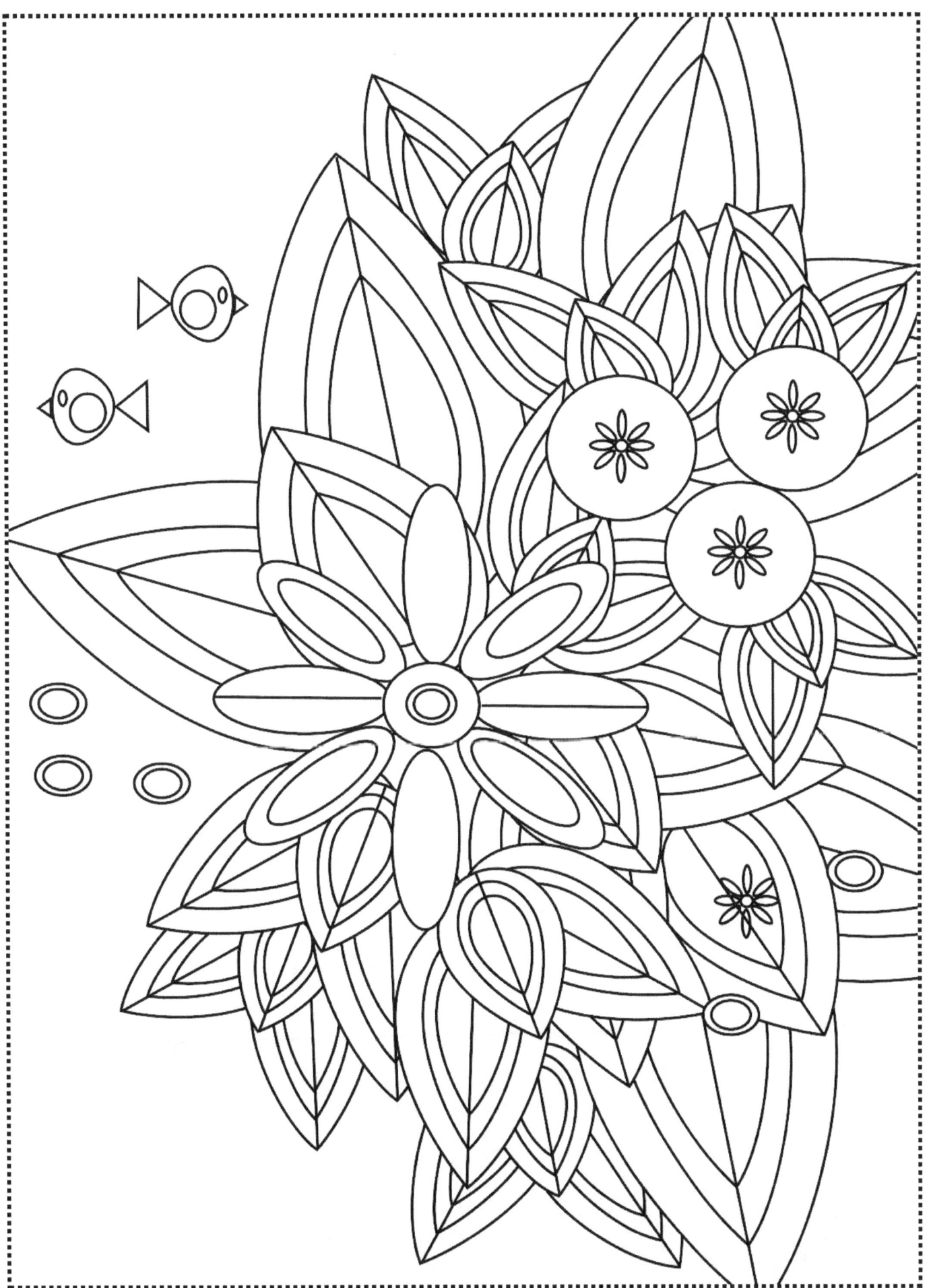

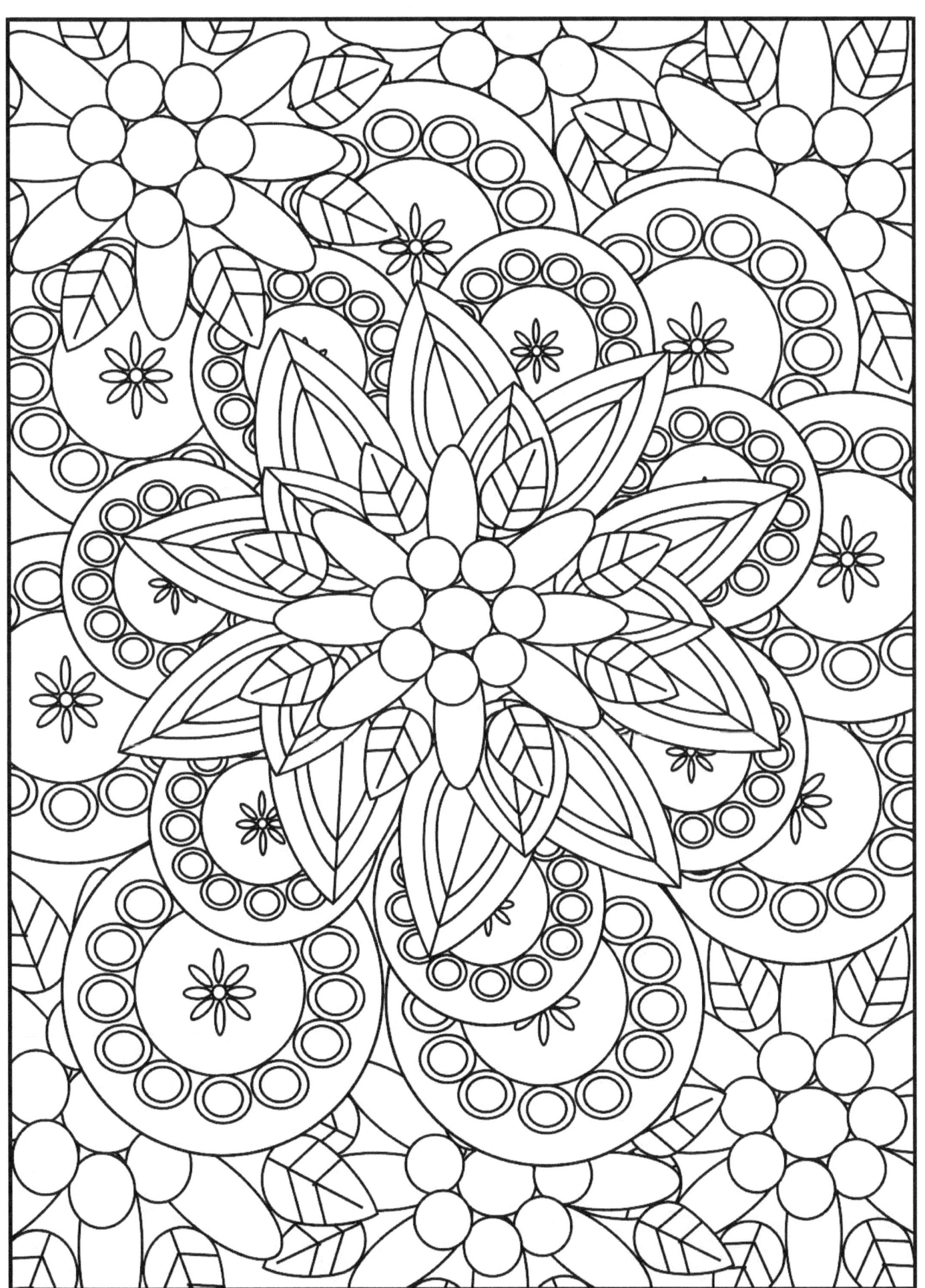

… Look at the cat in the next window! What is he thinking about? What is he dreaming about? …

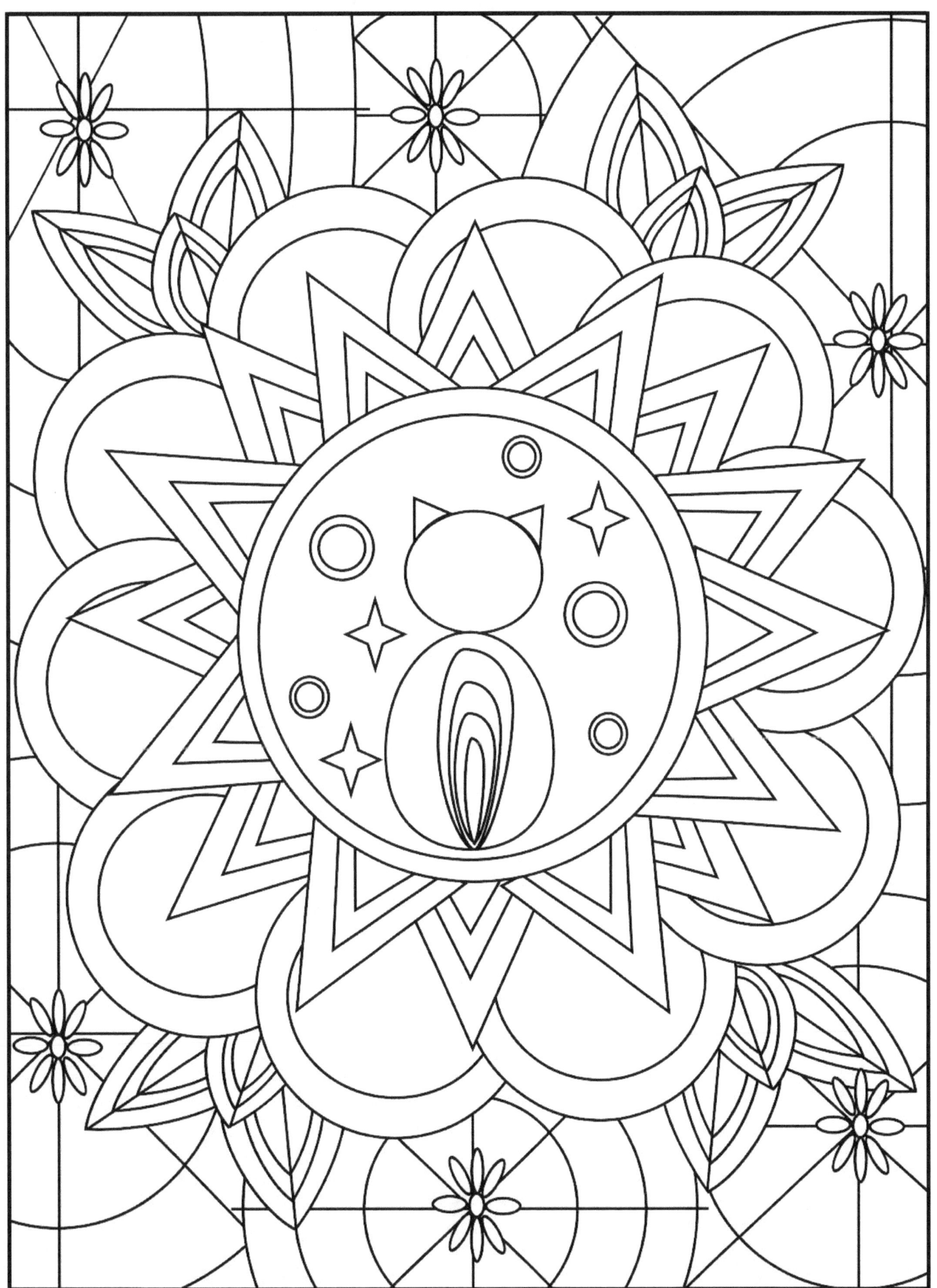

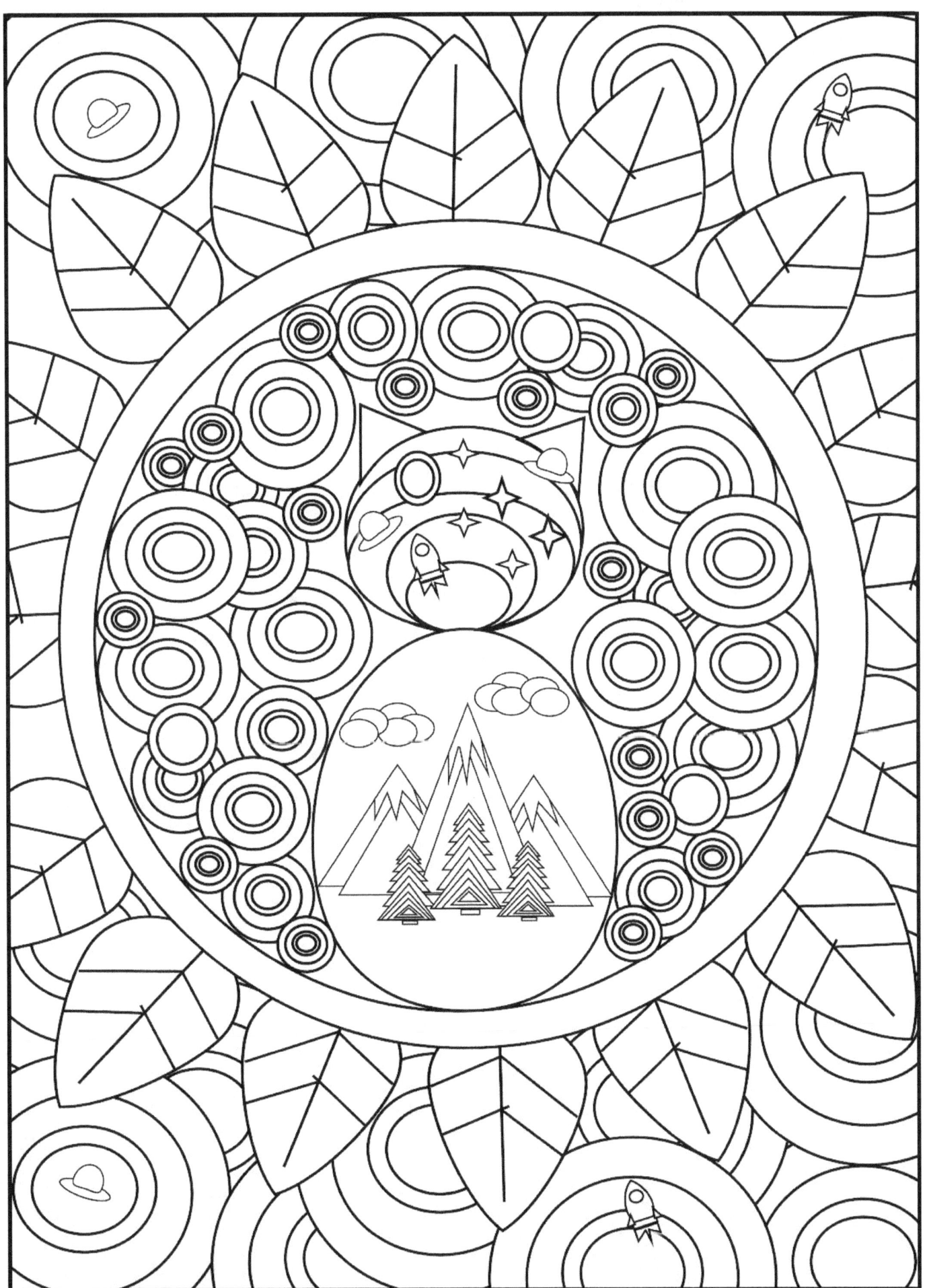

… Let's imagine space, other universes. What's life there like? …

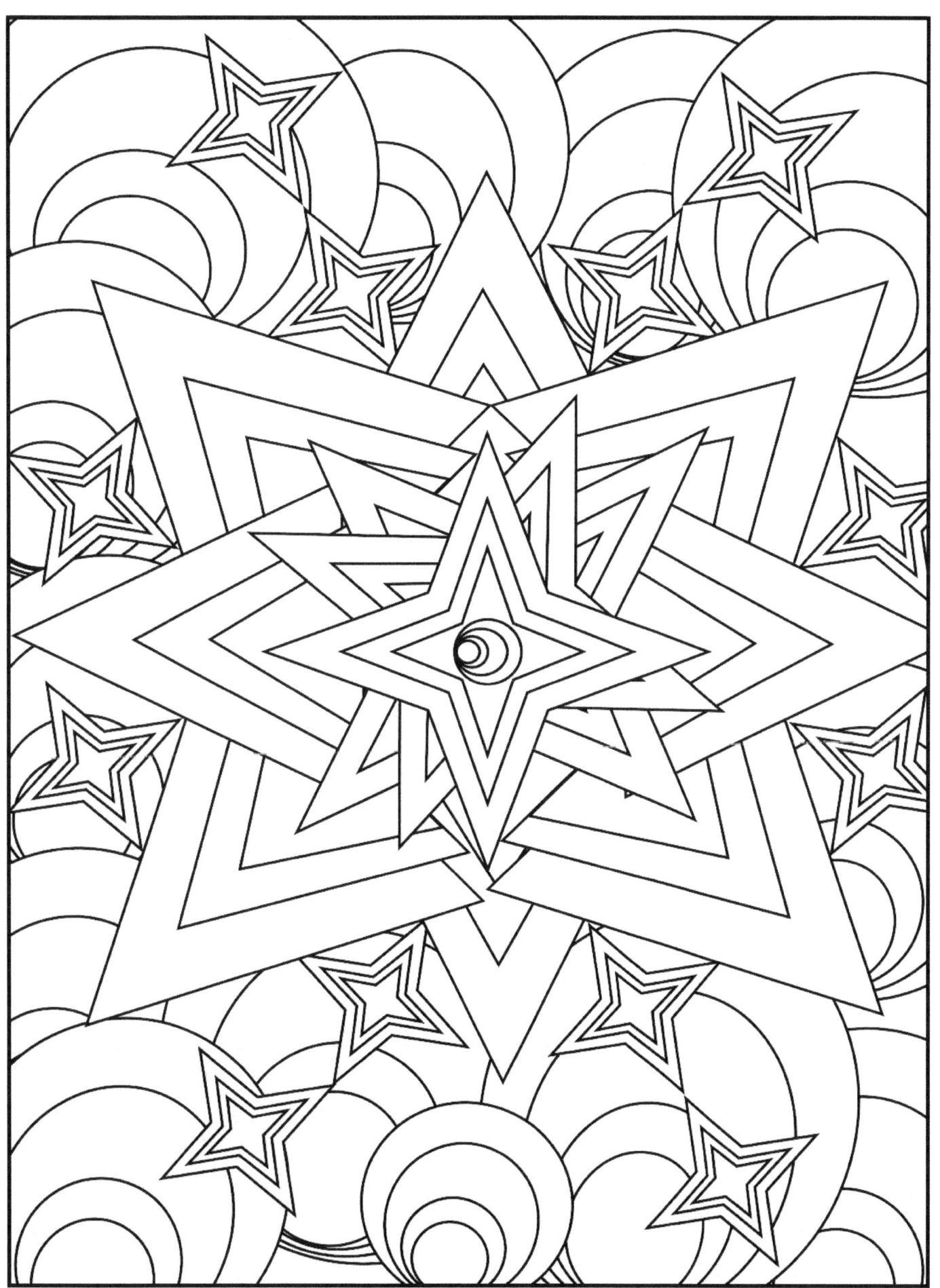

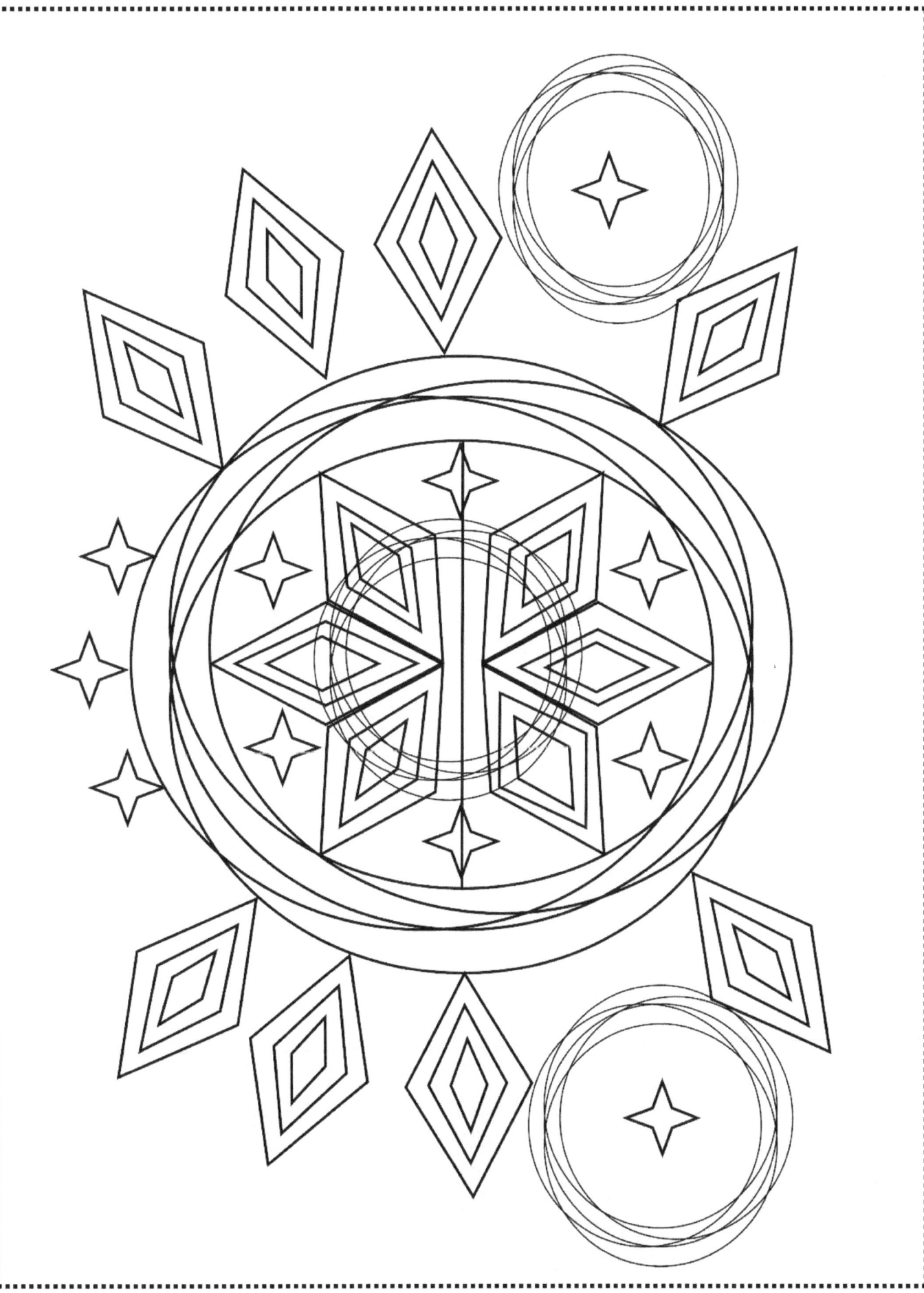

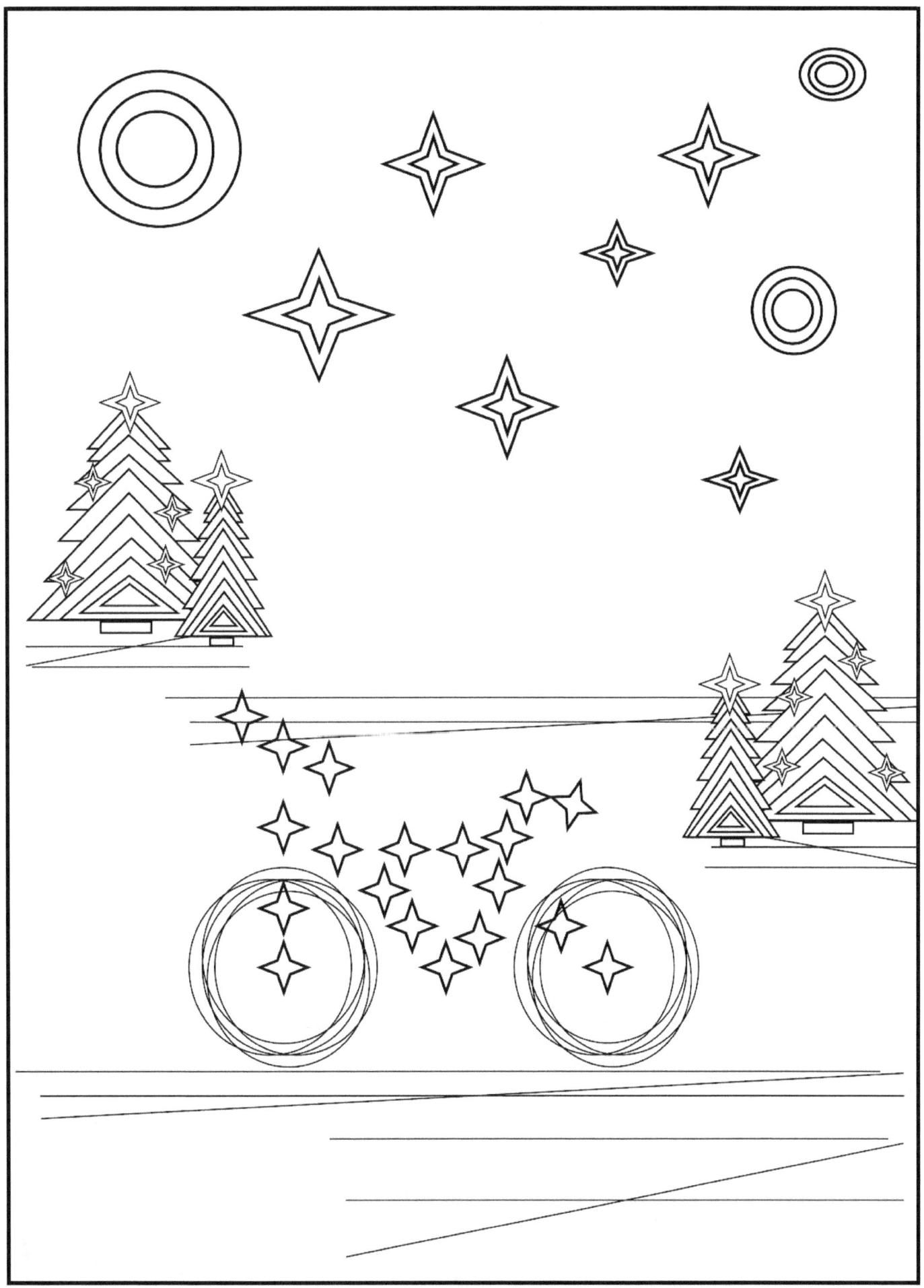

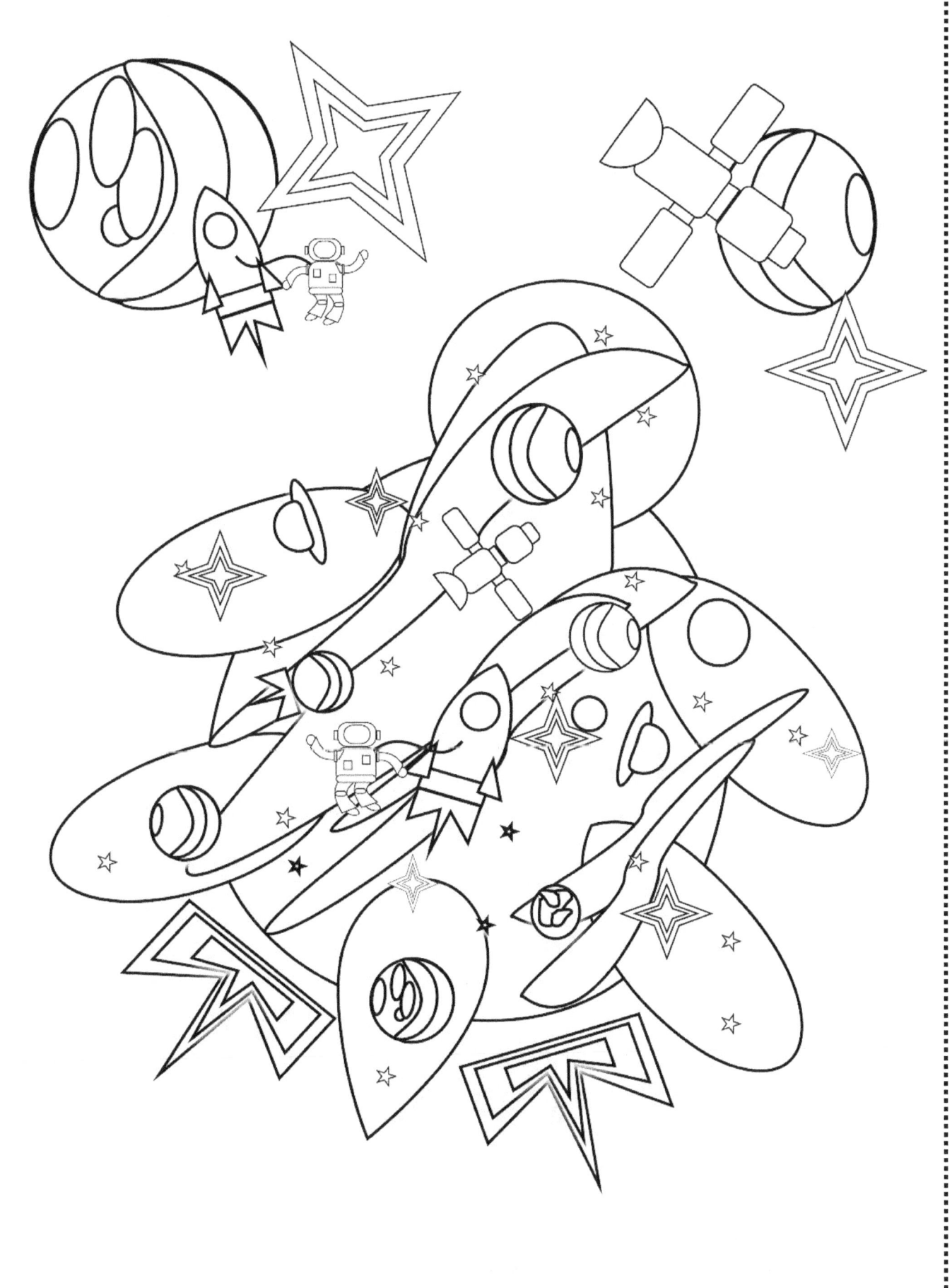

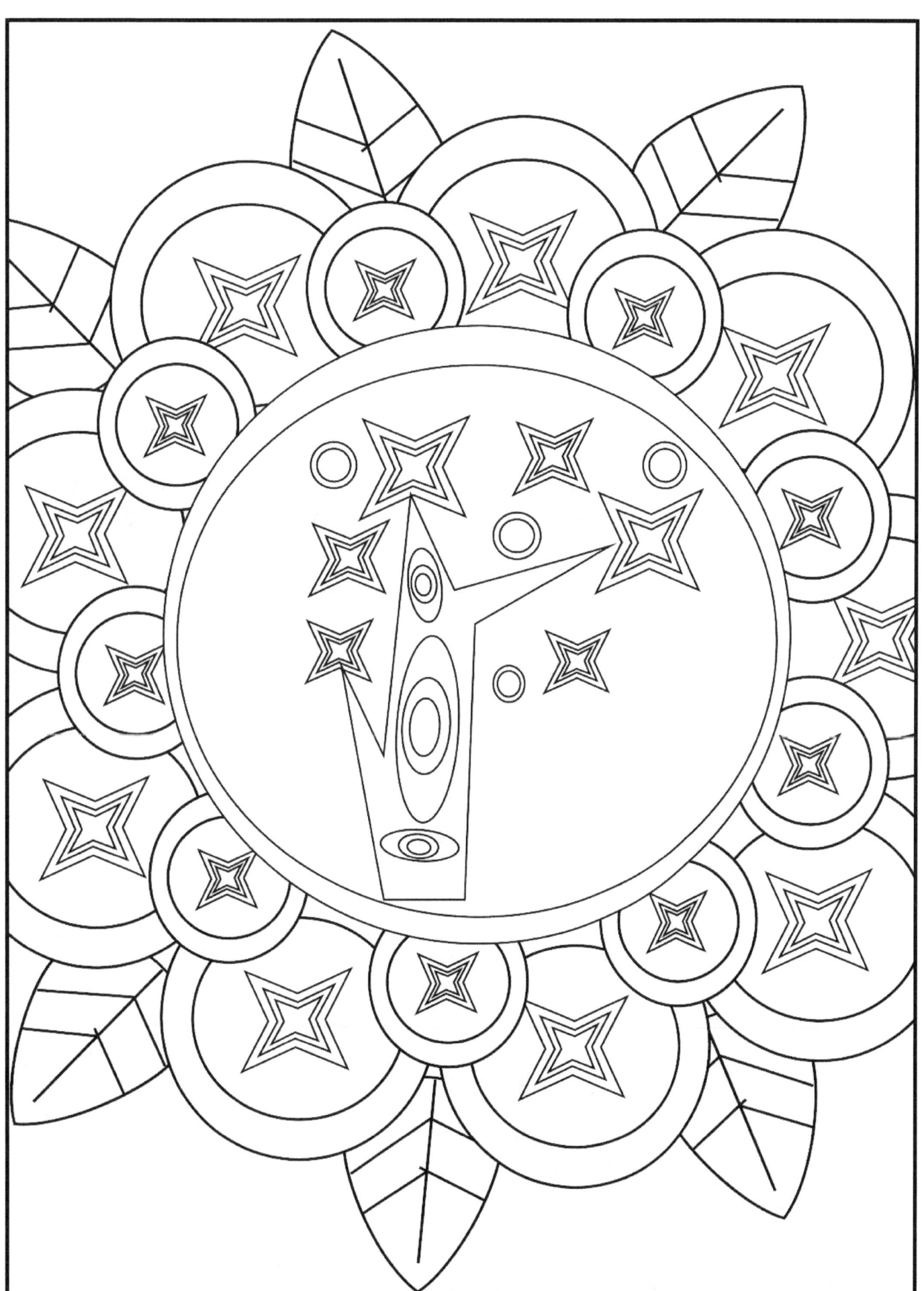

... Let's go back to our planet, go to the forest or park. Let's turn off the music and enjoy the silence. Let's take a break from the noisy city and listen to beautiful birdsong...

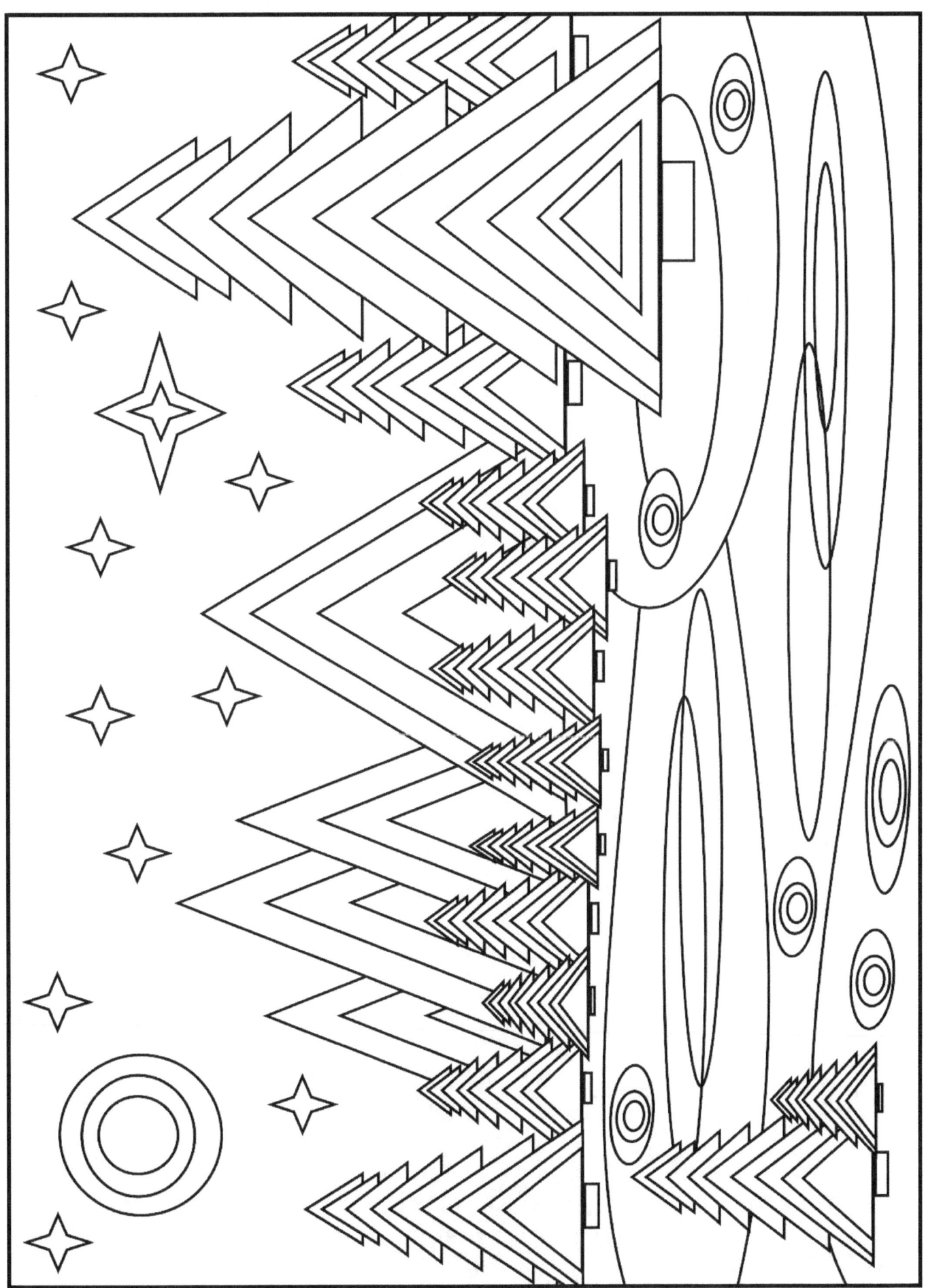

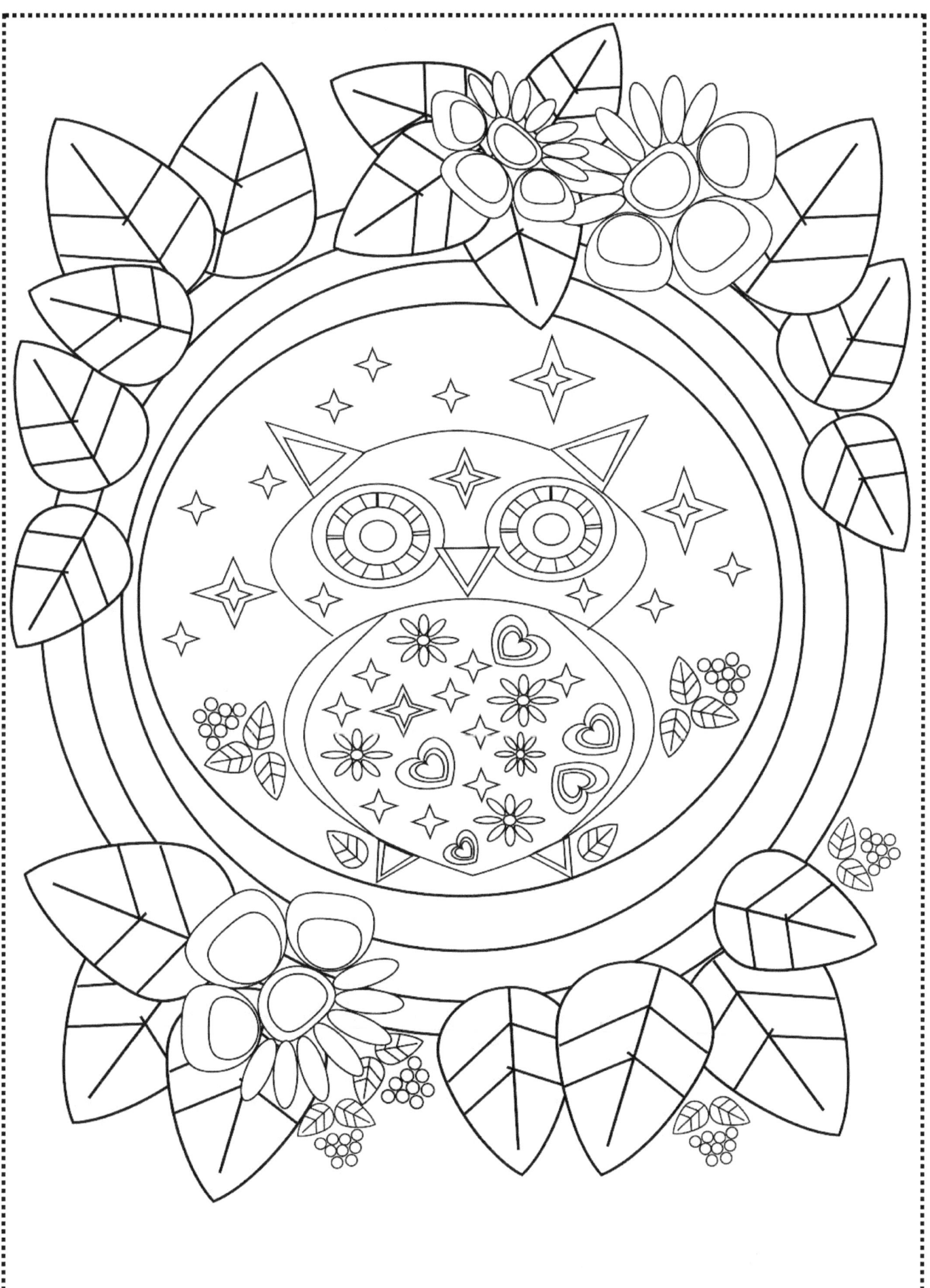

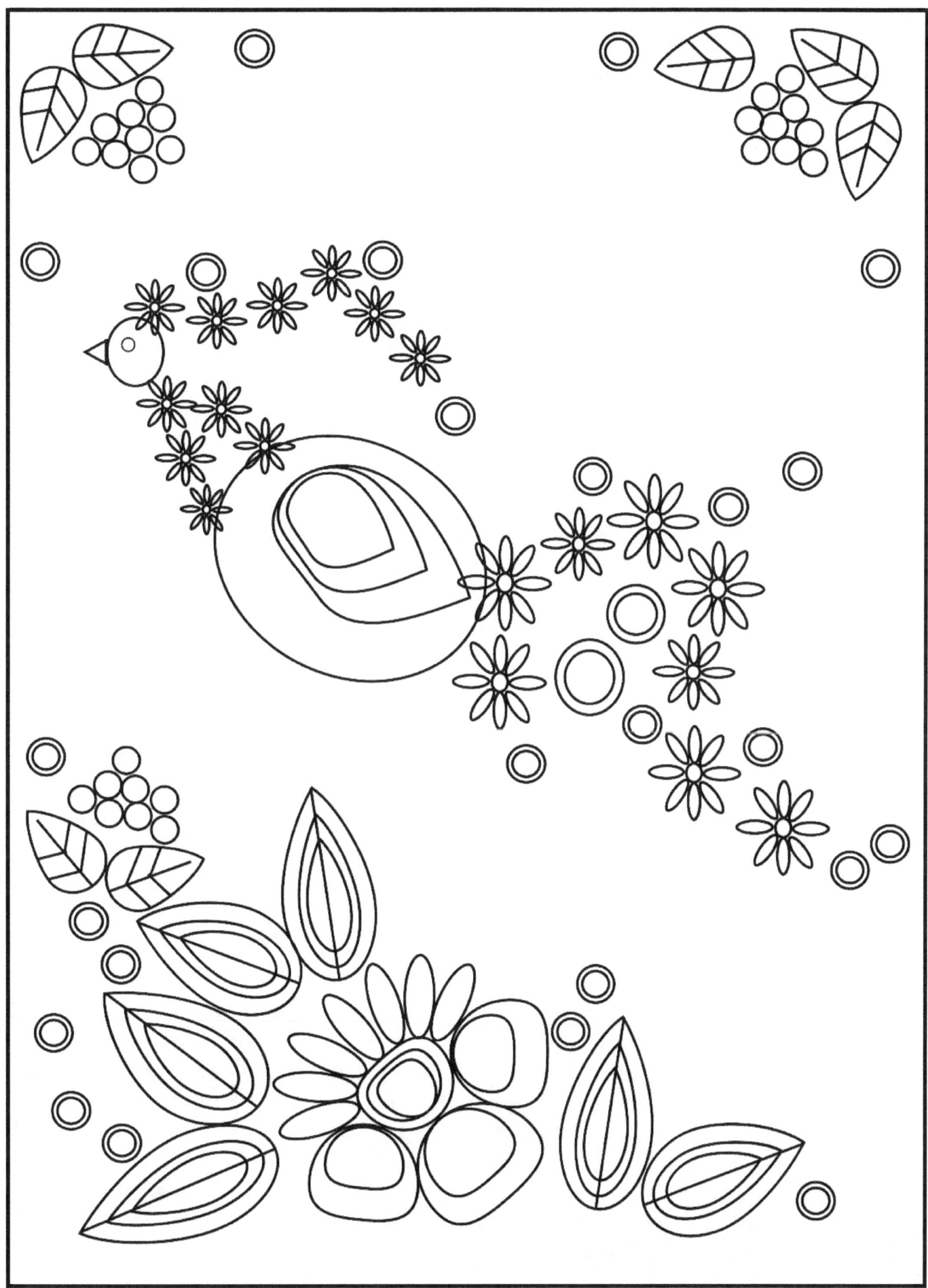

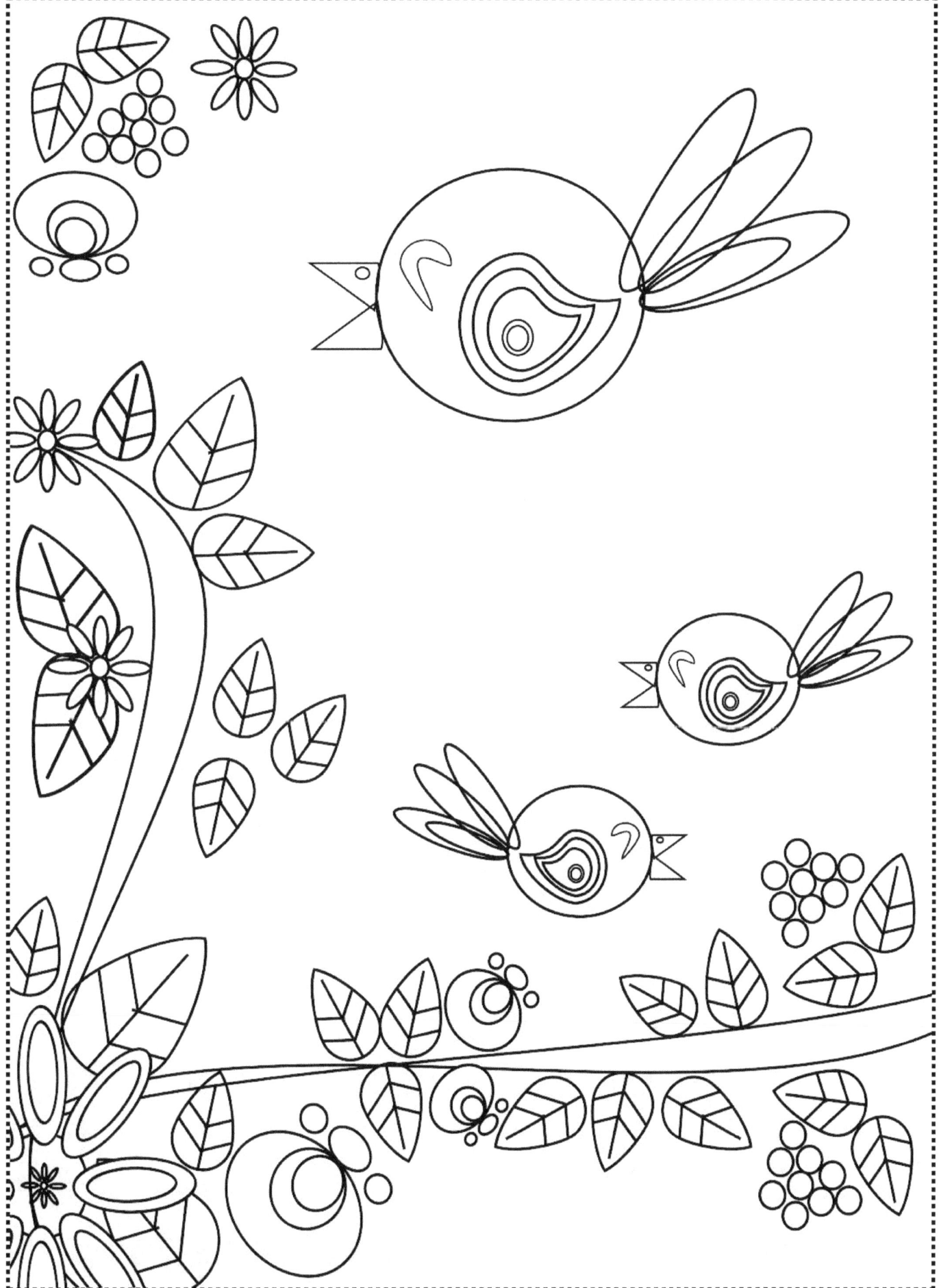

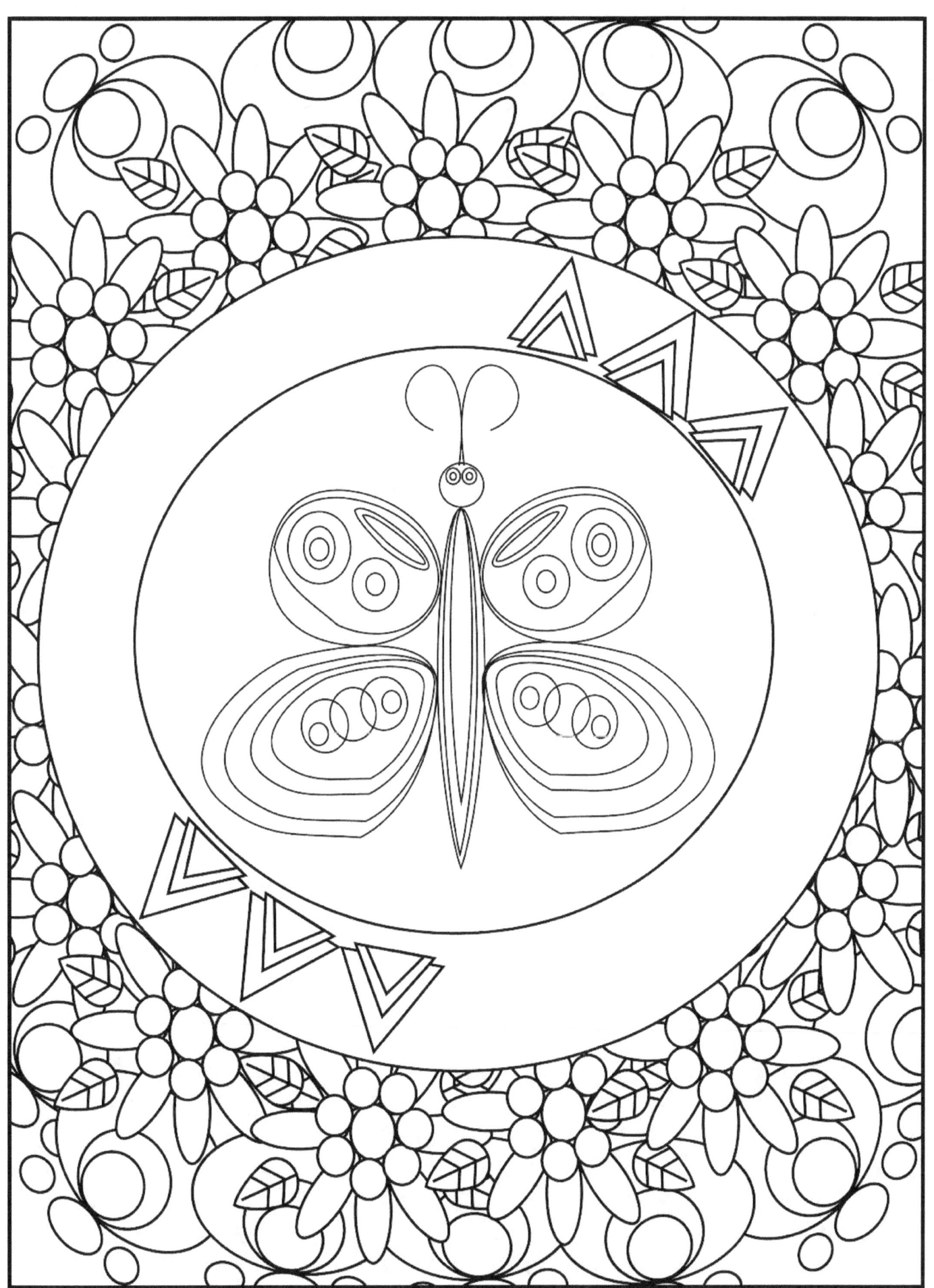

.... It is time to go home. We forgot to water the cacti! ...

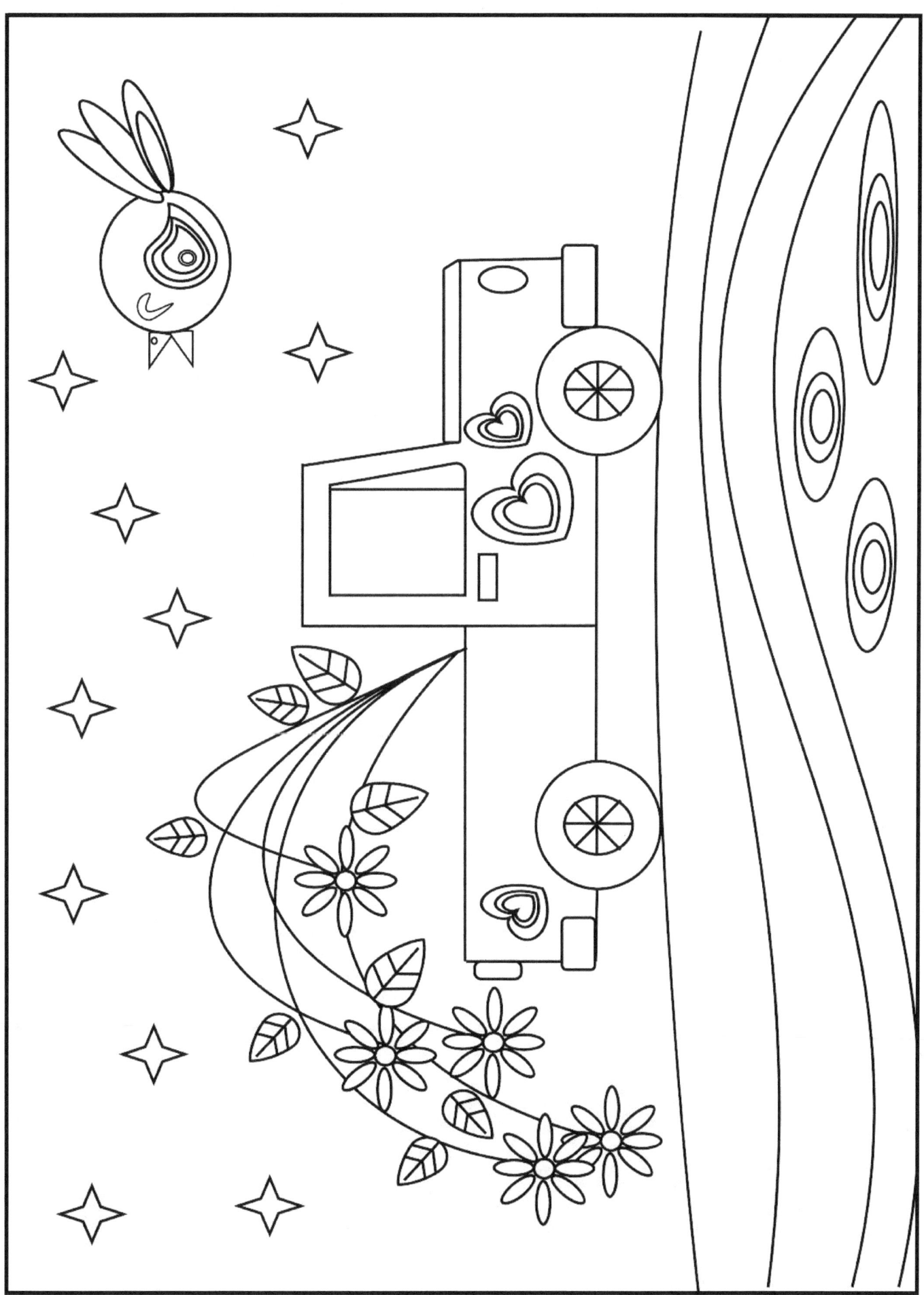

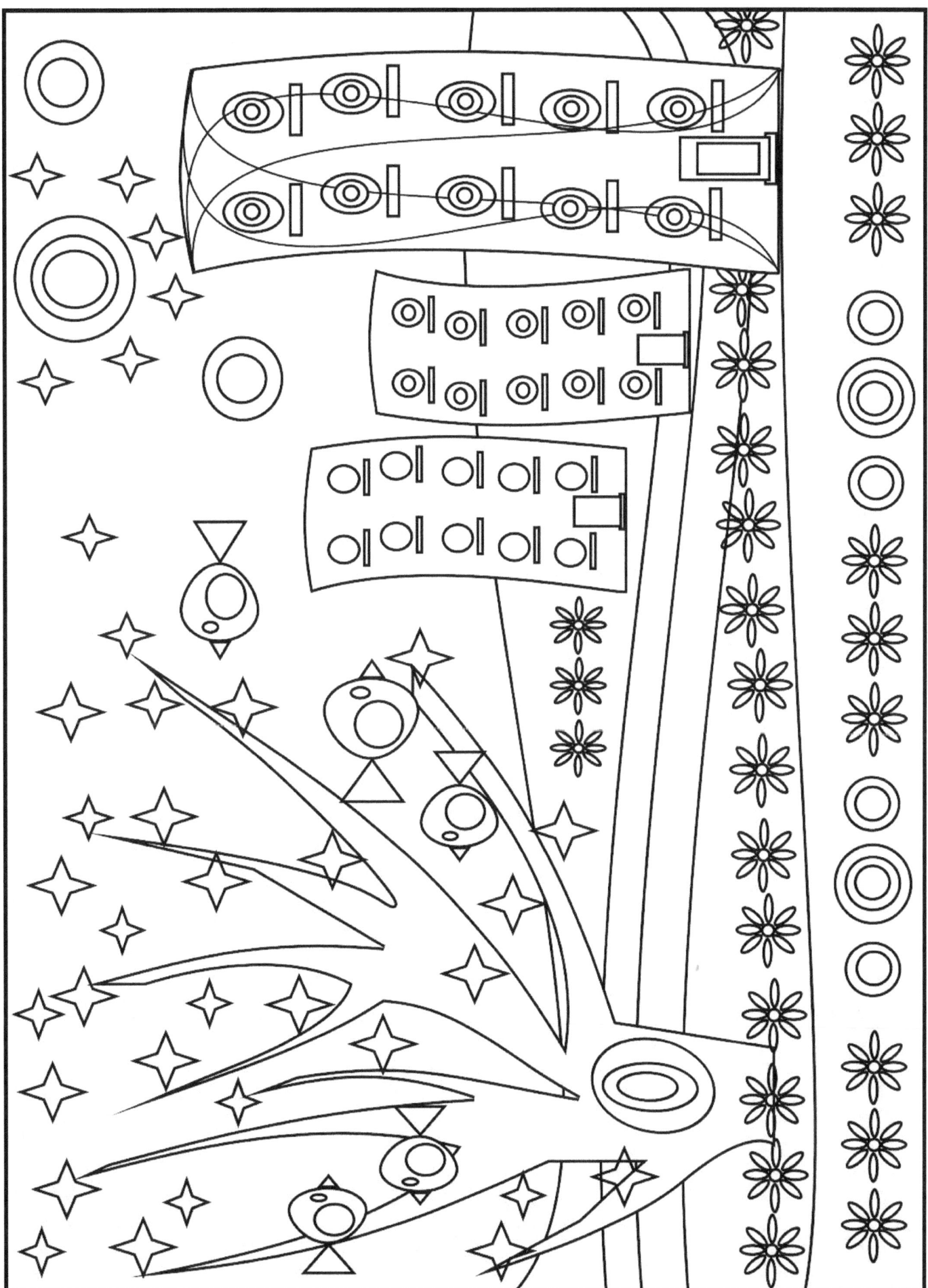

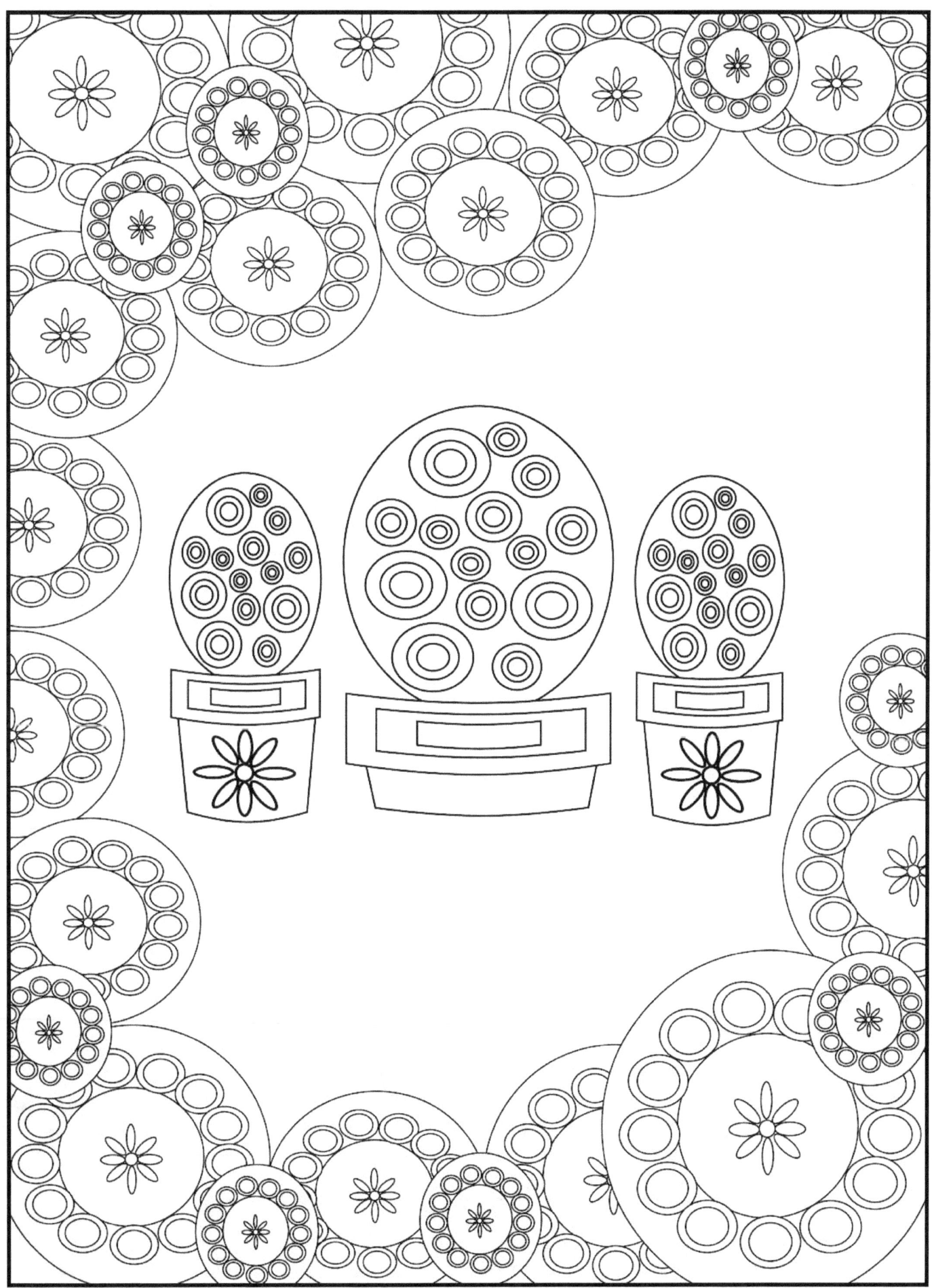

.... The cacti are happyThanks for a wonderful trip!.....

www.ingramcontent.com/pod-product-compliance
Lightning Source LLC
Chambersburg PA
CBHW081704220526
45466CB00009B/2879